Explore 360°

THE TOMB OF
TUTANKHAMUN

DISCOVER EGYPT'S GREATEST WONDER

Stella Caldwell

With illustrations by
Somchith Vongprachanh

BARRON'S

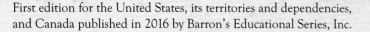

First edition for the United States, its territories and dependencies, and Canada published in 2016 by Barron's Educational Series, Inc.

Text, design, and illustration © copyright 2016 by Carlton Books Ltd.
Executive Editor: Selina Wood
Design: Rockjaw Creative
Design Manager: Emily Clarke
3-D Artists: Somchith Vongprachanh; Guido Salimbeni
Texture Artist: Drew McGovern
App Developers: Red Frog Digital Limited
Picture Research: Steve Behan
Production: Charlotte Larcombe
Design Director: Russell Porter
Publisher: Russell McLean
Historical Consultants: The Griffith Institute,
University of Oxford

All inquiries should be addressed to:
Barron's Educational Series, Inc.
250 Wireless Boulevard
Hauppauge, NY 11788
www.barronseduc.com

Product conforms to all applicable CPSC and CPSIA 2008 standards. No lead or phthalate hazard.

ISBN: 978-0-7641-6821-5

Library of Congress Control Number: 2015939644

Date of Manufacture: December 2015
Manufactured by: RRD Asia, China

Printed in China
9 8 7 6 5 4 3 2 1

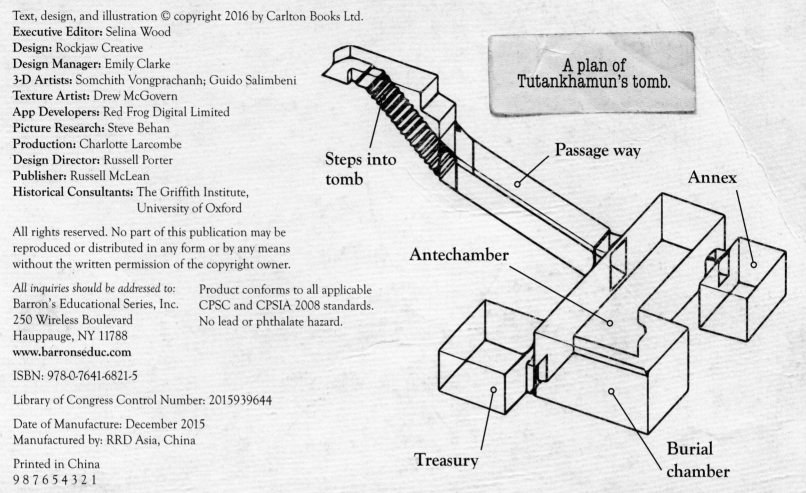

A plan of Tutankhamun's tomb.

Steps into tomb

Passage way

Annex

Antechamber

Treasury

Burial chamber

EXPLORE 360°

HOW TO USE THE APP:

1. Download the free **TutTomb 360** iOS App from the Apple App Store or Android App from Google Play. Open it to activate your device's camera.

2. View these pages (pp. 2–3) of the book though your device to begin your virtual tour.

3. Navigate the tomb using the directional button (see bottom left corner of screen) to move forward or back.

4. If your device has a built-in "gyroscope" feature, you can rotate the device through 360 degrees to view to the left or right and up or down. If not, you can swipe the screen with your finger to change the screen view and choose the direction you want to go in.

5. Tap objects inside the tomb, and some will reveal 3-D models. Rotate and pinch and zoom to discover amazing details. (Tap the return button, ←, to return to the virtual tour.)

Introduction

Tutankhamun was an Egyptian pharaoh who died in about 1323 B.C. The discovery of his nearly intact tomb by Howard Carter in 1922 is regarded as one of the most remarkable archaeological finds ever made.

We have recreated Tutankhamun's tomb and its treasures using **ultra-real 3-D graphics**, and now you can **navigate** yourself around the tomb using the **TutTomb 360** app. These amazing new views of the tomb are so real you won't believe your eyes!

SYSTEM REQUIREMENTS
APPLE DEVICES – iPhone 4S and above with iOS 6.0 min;
iPad2 and above with iOS 6.0 min; iPhone Touch 5th Gen.
and above with iOS 6.0 min.
ANDROID DEVICES – with both front and back cameras using
Android 4.0 and above. ARMv7 processors. Currently, INTEL-
based devices are not supported.

If you've got a problem, check out this web page:
www.carltonbooks.co.uk/icarltonbooks/TutTomb

3

Kingdom of the Nile

When Tutankhamun became pharaoh in the fourteenth century B.C., the ancient Egyptian civilization had already existed for 1,600 years. After his death, it continued to thrive for almost the same number of years. Ancient Egypt was a land rich in culture, art, and ideas, and its mysterious ruins and tombs continue to fascinate us today.

This simple map of ancient Egypt shows how the Nile River runs through the country and forms the Nile Delta in the north.

Ancient Kingdoms

The kingdom of Egypt was first united under one ruler, Narmer, around 3000 B.C. A succession of pharaohs ruled over the land for over 3,000 years. Historians divide ancient Egyptian history into three main periods: the Old Kingdom, the Middle Kingdom, and the New Kingdom.

A siltstone palette thought to depict the unification of Upper and Lower Egypt by King Narmer.

MEDITERRANEAN SEA

Rosetta

Nile Delta

LOWER EGYPT

Giza
Saqqara • Memphis

RED SEA

River Nile

Akhetaten (Amarna)

UPPER EGYPT

Deir el-Bahari

Valley of the Kings
Karnak
Thebes (Luxor)

Edfu
Abu Simbel

The last pharaoh, Cleopatra, was famous for her intellect, ambition, and beauty.

The Height of the Egyptian Empire

The Egyptian Empire reached its peak during the thirteenth century B.C. under the New Kingdom pharaoh Ramesses II. During its final 1,000 years, the empire was invaded several times, including by the Macedonians under Alexander the Great. In 30 B.C., after the death of the last pharaoh, Cleopatra, Egypt passed into Roman hands.

The importance of the Nile River in ancient Egypt is clear from the number of model boats, such as this one, which have been found in tombs.

The Black Land

Without the Nile River, there could have been no great civilization in Egypt. Each summer, the Nile flooded, leaving behind a black mud that fertilized the land, making it an ideal place to farm. The Egyptians believed that this miraculous event was the work of the gods. They called their country "Kemet," or the Black Land. On either side of the Nile River was a vast and barren desert known as "Deshret," or the Red Land.

Ramesses II became pharaoh in 1279 B.C. and is famous for building temples and monuments.

Thutmose III ruled from 1479 B.C. to 1425 B.C. and led successful military campaigns in western Asia.

Hatshepsut extended Egypt's trade links with neighboring powers, making Egypt wealthy, peaceful, and stable.

The Mighty Pharaohs

Egyptian pharaohs were believed to be "god-kings," filled with the divine power of the Egyptian god Horus. They were not considered to have the same power as the traditional gods, but neither were they seen as ordinary mortals. Most pharaohs ruled with supreme authority, though they were still expected to be just and merciful leaders.

Famous Pharaohs

While Tutankhamun is Egypt's most famous pharaoh, he was not its greatest. That honor probably belongs to Ramesses II, who reigned for 67 years and who built more monuments than any other pharaoh. Akhenaten–Tutankhamun' father–is famous, because, during his reign, he banished the traditional gods and only the sun god Aten was worshipped. Khufu is celebrated as the builder of the Great Pyramid, while Thutmose III conquered more land than any other pharaoh.

This tomb painting shows the pharaoh Sety I before the falcon-headed god Horus. All pharaohs were believed to be filled with Horus' spirit.

Royal Symbols

In Egyptian art, pharaohs are associated with certain symbols of power. The shepherd's crook stands for a king's role as protector, while a flail (a farming tool) represents the great fertility of his kingdom. Pharaohs are shown with a variety of crowns representing Upper and Lower Egypt, and are frequently seen wearing a striped nemes headdress with cobra and vulture heads on their foreheads.

This royal headdress features the cobra of Lower Egypt and vulture of Upper Egypt.

Pharaohs carried the symbols of the shepherd's crook and flail.

Ramesses II in his chariot at the Battle of Qadesh, fighting the Hittites.

Egypt at War

Pharaohs were trained as warriors and were expected to lead their armies into battle. By the time of the New Kingdom, Egypt had an impressive fighting force of foot soldiers and chariot troops. At the battle of Qadesh against the Hittites in 1274 B.C., Egyptian chariots were light and fast, with both a driver and a warrior armed with bow and arrow.

Hatshepsut

Only very rarely did women become pharaohs. Hatshepsut's rise to power was extraordinary. As the widow of Thutmose II, she was supposed to stand in as "regent" for her baby stepson, Thutmose III, until he was old enough to rule. However, the ambitious queen ended up proclaiming herself pharaoh and ruled for 20 years.

Hatshepsut built the famous Mortuary Temple at Deir el-Bahari, which was dedicated to the sun god Ra.

The Age of Pyramids

During the early Old Kingdom, pharaohs were buried in bench-shaped tombs called mastabas. However, when King Djoser built the Step Pyramid in 2630 B.C., this brought about a huge change in the way future pharaohs would be buried. Not only royal tombs, pyramids were also monuments that celebrated the great might of the pharaohs.

The First Pyramid

Built by Djoser's talented architect, Imhotep, the Step Pyramid was at first intended to be a mastaba tomb. However, Imhotep continued to add platforms to the tomb until finally there were six. Hidden beneath this giant stairway to the sky were Djoser's burial chamber and a maze of passages. Later, pharaoh Snefru built at least three pyramids. His so-called "Red Pyramid"—built from red limestone—was the first "true pyramid," because its sides sloped to a point.

The Step Pyramid at Saqqara is 205 feet (62 m) high and was the largest building of its time.

The Pyramids of Giza

The largest pyramid of all—the Great Pyramid—was built at Giza for the pharaoh Khufu over a 20-year period, concluding around 2560 B.C. It stands next to pyramids built later for his son Khafre and grandson Menkaure.

The pyramids at Giza: Khufu's Great Pyramid (top), the pyramid of Khafre (middle), and the pyramid of Menkaure (bottom).

Gods and Religion

The ancient Egyptians worshipped over 2,000 gods and goddesses. Some, like the sun god Ra, were important across Egypt. Others, such as the cat goddess Bastet, were only worshipped in certain areas. There was no one central dogma in Egyptian religion, and even the best-known myths had many versions.

Bastet was the goddess of fire, cats, the home, and pregnant women.

A relief on a tomb wall depicting the god Ra with the sun above his head.

Gods and Goddesses

Most Egyptian gods represented a particular aspect of the world, an activity, or an idea. Osiris was the god of the dead, while Anubis was the god of embalming and Thoth was the god of wisdom. Many deities were associated with a particular animal, and they were often depicted in more than one way. For example, Hathor, the goddess of motherhood, is sometimes shown as a cow, a woman, or a combination of the two.

King of the Gods

Ra, later fused with the popular god of Thebes, Amun, to become Amun-Ra, was the most important god in Egyptian religion and was believed to watch over all creation. By day, he sailed across the sky in "the Boat of Millions of Years," and, at night, traveled through the underworld in order to be born again for the new day.

Anubis was the god of funeral rites.

Thoth was the god of wisdom and patron of scribes.

Horus was the god of the sky. His spirit entered Egypt's pharaohs.

Mummies and the Afterlife

The ancient Egyptians went to great lengths to prepare for death and the afterlife. The most important parts of a person were known as the ka (life force) and the ba (soul). The Egyptians believed that as long as a dead body was preserved, then the ka and the ba could live forever.

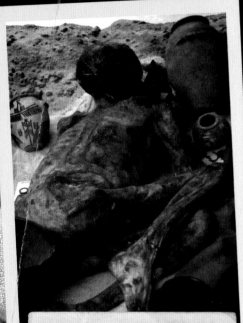

This natural, prehistoric mummy was buried in a sand-filled grave surrounded by grave goods.

The First Mummies

The earliest Egyptian mummies occurred naturally. Bodies were buried in the desert and preserved by the hot, dry sand. This happened because the bacteria that caused decay were unable to survive. As people began to be buried in coffins, the Egyptians looked for another way to preserve the body.

Anubis, the god of embalming and "friend of the dead," stands over an embalmed body.

Making a Mummy

The process of embalming took 70 days to complete. First, a body's vital organs were removed, apart from the treasured heart. The body was then covered in a salt called natron to dry it out and prevent decay, and left for 40 days. After this period, the body was stuffed with wads of linen and sand to give it shape.

Canopic Jars

The body's vital organs, apart from the discarded brain, were embalmed separately and placed in stone or pottery containers called canopic jars. Each jar was protected by one of the four sons of the god Horus.

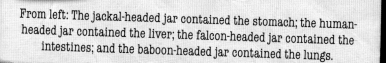

From left: The jackal-headed jar contained the stomach; the human-headed jar contained the liver; the falcon-headed jar contained the intestines; and the baboon-headed jar contained the lungs.

The inner coffin of Henutmehyt, a wealthy Egyptian woman. It is covered in gold leaf and shows the unfurled wings of the sky goddess Nut.

"As much as possible of the brain is extracted through the nostrils with an iron hook…"
Herodotus, who visited Egypt in about 450 B.C.

Coffins

The Egyptians believed the coffin was a sacred container that protected the body and ensured its survival in the afterlife. The coffin was also thought to display an idealized representation of the deceased. A rich person might have several beautifully decorated coffins, one inside another. They were usually made of painted or gilded wood.

Next, the body was coated in oils and resin to help protect the skin. Finally, the mummy was wrapped in layers of linen bandages and its face covered with a mask.

The unwrapped mummified body of pharaoh Ramesses II.

Wonder of the Ancient World

The incredible size of the Great Pyramid continues to astonish sightseers. Built from about 2.3 million blocks of stone (weighing an average of 2.525 tons (2.5 tonnes)); the pyramid was 485 feet (147 m) tall. It is still the largest stone building on Earth. One of the great mysteries of the ancient world is how exactly builders lifted the heavy slabs. Workers may have had ramps and levers of some kind, but they certainly had no pulleys or other machinery.

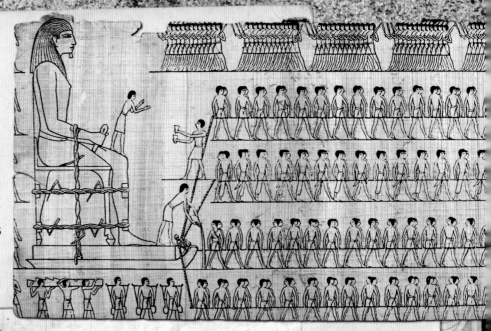

Inside the Pyramid

A maze of tunnels lies within the Great Pyramid. Experts think there are many tunnels, because the builders kept changing their minds about where to put the burial chamber. Although the pharaoh's sarcophagus remains in place in the king's chamber, the tomb's precious contents were stolen by thieves in antiquity.

This drawing shows workers pulling a huge statue. Water is being poured on the sand in front of the statue to make it easier to pull.

The Great Sphinx, a strange beast with the head of a pharaoh and the body of a lion, sits in front of the pyramid of Khafre.

Cross-section of the Great Pyramid
1. Underground burial chamber
2. Queen's chamber
3. King's chamber
4. Shafts
5. Weight-relieving chambers
6. Grand gallery
7. Well shaft
8. Entrance

The Eye of Horus

Charms and amulets were worn to protect both the living and dead from harm. The eyes of the falcon-headed god Horus were said to be the sun and the moon, and so the "Eye of Horus" became a particularly powerful amulet.

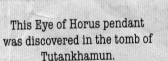

This Eye of Horus pendant was discovered in the tomb of Tutankhamun.

Worshipping the Gods

The great temples of Egypt were dedicated to the important gods, but only pharaohs and priests could worship within them. Ordinary people could pray outside the temples, or worship at the shrines of lesser gods. Many people had shrines within their homes dedicated to ancestors, or to gods such as Bes who protected the home.

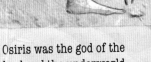

Bes protected homes and families against evil spirits.

Osiris was the god of the dead and the underworld.

Isis was the wife of Osiris and the goddess of fertility and magic.

Ra was the god of the sun and creation.

Seth was Osiris' brother and the god of darkness and chaos.

The Book of the Dead

The Egyptians believed that the underworld was fraught with danger—before they could reach the afterlife, the dead had to pass by lakes of fire and fearsome monsters. Magic spells were often written on papyri, coffins, or tomb walls. These texts—now known as *The Book of the Dead*—held the key to surviving the dangers of the underworld.

Devourer of the Dead

In the Hall of Two Truths, a person's heart was weighed against the feather of Maat, the goddess of truth. If a person had not led an honest and good life, the heart was judged to be too heavy. Then the crocodile-headed Ammit, "Devourer of the Dead," consumed the heart, and the soul was refused entry to the afterlife.

God of the Dead

The Egyptians told of how Osiris—who had once been king of Egypt—was murdered by his brother, Seth. Cutting the corpse up, Seth scattered the parts across Egypt. Osiris' wife, Isis, transformed herself into a bird of prey and found all but one of the body parts. With the help of the gods Anubis and Thoth, all these pieces were wrapped in cloth and laid out in the shape of Osiris. Isis kissed the mummy, and Osiris was reborn as god of the underworld.

The Opening of the Mouth Ceremony

This important ritual allowed the senses of a dead person to be "freed" so they could be useful in the afterlife. At the door of the tomb, the mummy was placed in an upright position and a priest used sacred tools to touch its face.

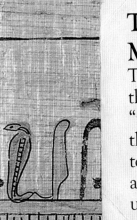

The Valley of the Kings

Tomb burglars ransacked the pyramids of Old and Middle Kingdom pharaohs; therefore, during the New Kingdom, a different burial tradition began. The Valley of the Kings lies west of the Nile in a remote desert valley opposite Thebes (modern-day Luxor), and it was here that pharaohs were buried in secret rock-cut tombs.

A Royal Cemetery

For a period of 500 years, nearly every New Kingdom pharaoh was buried in the Valley of the Kings. Most tombs had deep corridors descending through one or more rooms to the burial chamber. Here, in the "House of Gold," pharaohs were buried with their riches. The tombs' narrow entrances could be easily guarded; but, despite this, only Tutankhamun's tomb escaped being completely looted by thieves.

The Valley of the Kings was chosen for its isolation, but tomb burglars were still able to loot almost all the tombs.

The Tomb of Sety I

The magnificent tomb of Sety I was discovered by Giovanni Battista Belzoni in 1817. It is the longest of any of the tombs in the valley, and its walls are beautifully painted. In 2010, archaeologists discovered that a mysterious tunnel descending deep into the rock comes to an abrupt end. Perhaps Sety intended for another burial chamber to be built, but died before the work could be completed.

Sety I stands between the gods Osiris (left) and Horus (right) in one of the paintings from his tomb.

A magnificent painting of Maat, goddess of truth, from the tomb of Nefertari.

The Valley of the Queens

The wives of pharaohs were buried close to their husbands in the Valley of the Queens. In ancient times, it was called Ta-Set-Neferu, or "the place of beauty." Nefertari, the favorite wife of Ramesses II, was buried here—her tomb is considered to be one of ancient Egypt's finest.

Deir el-Medina

In the 1920s, archaeologists uncovered the ancient remains of a tomb artisans' village near the Valley of the Kings. Called Deir el-Medina, the village flourished for 500 years and consisted of around 70 narrow houses crammed together.

The ruins of Deir el-Medina have much to tell us about everyday Egyptian life.

A stool and broom found at Deir el-Medina.

The Great Temples

The magnificent temples that stood along the banks of the Nile were built as dwelling places for the gods. Although much of Egyptian life revolved around these temples, only pharaohs and priests were allowed to worship within them.

Sacred Rituals

A statue of the temple's god was kept in the dark, innermost sanctuary. Here, sacred rituals were carried out three times a day: priests washed and dressed the god's statue, incense was burned, and food and drink were offered. When they left at night, the priests swept away their footsteps to remove all human traces.

Karnak

The temple of Karnak at Thebes (modern-day Luxor)—sacred to the god Amun-Ra—is the biggest temple still standing in Egypt. The temple's construction began during the Middle Kingdom, but continued through the New Kingdom and beyond—successive pharaohs continued to add more statues and courtyards. Karnak became the most important religious center in the land: to the Egyptians it was known as "the most perfect of places."

As religion was an important part of Egyptian life, priests were highly regarded in Egyptian society.

The vast columns in the Great Hypostyle Hall at Karnak Temple are covered in hieroglyphs (ancient Egyptian script).

The temple of Edfu was dedicated to the falcon-headed god, Horus.

Religious Festivals

Ordinary Egyptians were only allowed as far as the temple gates. However, on certain days of the year, festivals were held to honor the gods. On these occasions, their statues would be paraded on their sacred boats outside their temples in processions accompanied by the shaven-headed priests.

Remembered in Stone

The greatest building project of the mighty pharaoh Ramesses II was the two magnificent rock-cut temples at Abu Simbel. The Small Temple was dedicated to the goddess Hathor and Ramesses' wife Nefertari, while the Great Temple was sacred to Amun-Ra, Ra-Horakhty, Ptah, and Ramesses himself. Gazing out across the Nile, four towering statues, or colossi, of Ramesses flank the entrance to the Great Temple.

The four massive statues of Ramesses II at his temple at Abu Simbel.

Everyday Life

Most Egyptians lived close to the Nile, as its fertile valley was perfect for farming and fishing. The river also provided a highway linking Egyptian cities, and it bustled with all kinds of vessels, from small cargo boats to ships bearing huge stone obelisks.

Food and Drink

The Egyptians enjoyed a varied diet. Wheat and barley were used to make bread and beer, and grapes were plucked for wine making. Farmers grew many vegetables and fruits, and the Nile provided plentiful fish for everyone. Meat, however, was considered to be a luxury.

This tomb painting shows an Egyptian farmer plowing the fields.

This beautiful painting shows wealthy Egyptian official Nebamun hunting birds on the marshes of the Nile.

A model of a typical Egyptian home dating from around 4,000 years ago.

Egyptian Homes

Houses were made of mud brick and were whitewashed to keep out the heat. In crowded cities, homes were built two or three storeys high. Furniture was a luxury—those who could afford it had low chairs and tables carved from local wood and mud-brick beds. Rich Egyptians lived in luxurious villas with pretty gardens.

Beauty and Finery

Most clothing was made from cool, white linen, and varied from simple dresses to extravagant robes. Both men and women used eye makeup, and the rich often wore wigs of human hair. The Egyptians loved beauty and adorned themselves in jewelry, in life and death.

This stunning necklace was found on the mummy of Psusennes I.

Childhood

Boys from wealthier families attended school, while girls stayed at home and learned how to run a household. Children played with many different toys, from clay balls to spinning tops and model animals.

A wooden toy cat with moving jaw and bronze teeth dating from 1550-1070 B.C.

Queen Nefertari, the wife of Ramesses II, plays the board game senet.

Parties and Leisure

Scenes from tomb walls reveal that the Egyptians loved parties. The wealthy held extravagant banquets, with delicacies such as gazelle and ostrich on the menu. Musicians would entertain guests with harps and lyres, and entertainers danced, sang, and performed acrobatics. In their spare time, people loved to play the board game senet—Tutankhamun was buried with four senet boards.

Hieroglyphs

Hieroglyphs were a complicated writing system with around 700 different signs. The Egyptians used this system to inscribe monuments, temples, and tombs, and a special form called hieratic was used for writing on papyrus scrolls. It is thanks to the decipherment of this code by Jean-Francois Champollion in 1822 that we know so much about ancient Egypt today.

Champollion, the man who unlocked hieroglyphs, is often called the Father of Egyptology.

Picture Writing

Most hieroglyphs stand for sounds and can be roughly matched to a consonant letter in our alphabet. For example, the owl symbol stands for the letter "M." Some symbols stand for a whole word—for instance, the open mouth symbol may mean "mouth," though it also represents the letter "R."

Egypt's Lost Language

For centuries, people struggled to make sense of Egypt's forgotten language. Without being able to read the mysterious symbols found on ancient monuments, explorers could tell very little about their discoveries. Then, in 1798, Napoleon's soldiers discovered a slab of black stone at Rosetta on Egypt's Mediterranean coast. It had three scripts on it: one in Greek and two in Egyptian. Here at last was the code to hieroglyphs.

The Rosetta stone was discovered at Fort Julien, near Rosetta, by one of Napoleon's French troops.

Unlocking the Code

The first 14 lines on the Rosetta Stone are hieroglyphs, the middle section is "demotic" (a cursive version of hieroglyphs), and the last section is Greek. Champollion realized that the scripts were translations of each other, and by comparing them was able to decipher two pharaohs' names: Ptolemy and Cleopatra. This allowed him to gradually work out hieroglyphs for all the Greek words on the stone—and to finally crack the code.

The Rosetta Stone was inscribed with a decree issued in 196 B.C. by pharaoh Ptolemy V.

This painted limestone sculpture of an Egyptian scribe is about 4,500 years old.

Scribes

Scribes were experts in writing, and members of one of the noblest professions in ancient Egypt. The training was tough, however, and scribes were schooled for many years from a young age. For everyday writing on papyri, scribes used a faster version of hieroglyphs called hieratic, while demotic, an even faster, or later, version of hieratic, was often used for legal documents.

Egypt's Lost Treasures

After the decline of ancient Egyptian civilization, its splendid treasures were gradually forgotten. It was only after the discovery of the Rosetta Stone and the decipherment of hieroglyphs that the science known as Egyptology—the study of ancient Egypt—was truly born.

Early Adventurers

The reckless enthusiasm of early explorers caused much damage to ancient sites. One of these adventurers, Giovanni Belzoni, had originally been a circus strongman—he was 6 feet (1.8 m) tall, and once became wedged in one of the Great Pyramid's tiny passageways! Belzoni was hired to remove the colossal head of Ramesses II from the Ramesseum and ship it to the British Museum in England. He also cleared the temples at Abu Simbel and discovered the tomb of Sety I in the Valley of the Kings.

It took 130 men 17 days to drag the huge bust of Ramesses II to the Nile for shipping.

Italian explorer and archaeologist Giovanni Belzoni (1778-1823).

Digging at Saqqara

The French archaeologist Auguste Mariette was first sent to Egypt to acquire ancient manuscripts, but he instead started digging at Saqqara. Here, he unearthed the massive underground complex containing the burials of the sacred Apis bulls, today known as the Serapeum. Mariette later set up the Egyptian Museum in Cairo so that new discoveries could be kept in Egypt, where they belonged.

Apis bulls were mummified and then buried at the Serapeum at Saqqara (right).

The sacred Apis bull was worshipped by the Egyptians as a god of strength and fertility.

Modern Methods

It was William Matthew Flinders Petrie who introduced the careful excavation methods used by modern archaeologists. Petrie was very critical of the careless work of his predecessors—he realized that even the tiniest pottery fragments could reveal something about Egypt's history, and he meticulously recorded everything he found.

Flinders Petrie discovered this stela in 1896 at Thebes. It tells of the military victories of Egyptian king Merneptah.

Rescuing Abu Simbel

Today, Egyptology is not just about making new discoveries—it is also about careful preservation. In the 1960s, an amazing conservation project took place before the construction of the High Dam at Aswan. Since the Abu Simbel temples would have been flooded by the dam, they were cut into blocks, moved 215 feet (65 m) up the cliff face, and then carefully reconstructed like a giant jigsaw puzzle.

The statues from Abu Simbel temples were lifted up the cliff face, away from rising waters.

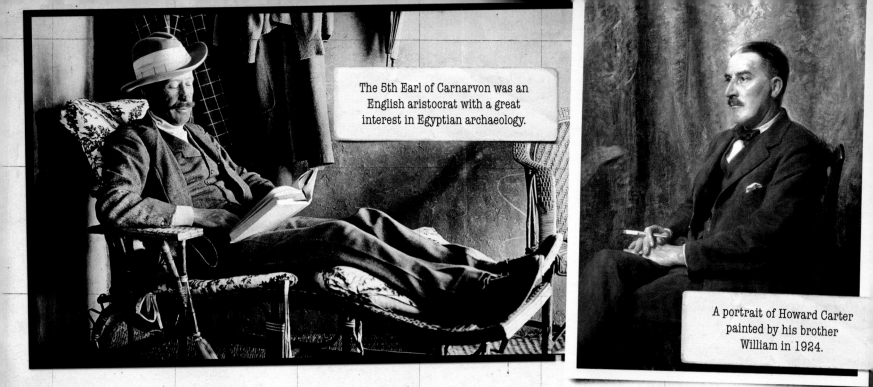

The 5th Earl of Carnarvon was an English aristocrat with a great interest in Egyptian archaeology.

A portrait of Howard Carter painted by his brother William in 1924.

Tutankhamun's Lost Tomb

Howard Carter's discovery of Tutankhamun's tomb in 1922 is surely the most exciting archaeological find ever made. Financed by Lord Carnarvon, Carter searched the Valley of the Kings for several years before finding the pharaoh's burial place.

The Valley of the Kings

In 1898, archaeologists began to excavate the Valley of the Kings seriously. Only one team of archaeologists could work there at a time—from 1902 to 1914, that permit belonged to the American Theodore Davis. Around 30 tombs were excavated during this period, though tomb burglars had looted all of them. In 1912, Davis announced, "I fear the Valley of the Tombs is now exhausted." The permit passed to Lord Carnarvon in 1915.

Theodore Davis (second from right) and other archaeologists in the Valley of the Kings in 1907.

This collar, made with flower petals, leaves and beads, was found among Tutankhamun's embalming items in 1907.

Vital Clues

Carnarvon and Carter were convinced that Tutankhamun lay buried in the valley. Davis had made two important finds. In 1907, a pit was discovered containing items used by ancient embalmers. Tutankhamun's name was inscribed on some of these objects. Two years later, a small chamber was discovered—in it was a wooden box containing gold leaf embossed with the name of Tutankhamun, as well as the names of his wife, Ankhesenamun, and his successor, Ay.

A photograph of Howard Carter's excavations, taken in early 1920, showing local people clearing the site.

The Search Begins

Due to the First World War (1914–1918), serious excavation work could not begin until 1917. Over the following years, thousands of tons of sand and rock were shifted with little progress made. By the summer of 1922, Carnarvon was growing impatient and told Carter he wanted to halt work. However, there was still one small area—near the tomb of Ramesses VI—that had yet to be searched. Carter persuaded Carnarvon to agree to one more season of digging.

"The Valley of the Tombs of the Kings— the very name is full of romance…"
Howard Carter

Carter's plan of the Valley of the Kings, showing the area between the tombs of Ramesses VI and Ramesses IX.

Red circle = where the tomb of Tutankhamun was found.

The Boy King

Tutankhamun was buried in the Valley of the Kings around 1323 B.C. Over the following centuries, his name was all but forgotten. It was only due to Carter's discovery of his tomb that he is now the most famous of all Egypt's pharaohs.

A Brief Reign

Tutankhamun became pharaoh when he was just eight or nine years old and was about 18 when he died. It is likely that high officials ruled on his behalf for much of his reign—upon his death, an official named Ay took his place. Tutankhamun's small tomb suggests he died suddenly and was hastily buried, though the precise cause of his death is still hotly debated.

A wooden box in the form of a cartouche (or ornate frame) containing the name of Tutankhamun.

A gilded statue of Tutankhamun with a spear was found in his tomb.

This scene from Tutankhamun's throne shows the king with his wife and sister, Ankhesenamun.

Tutankhamun's Family

Genetic tests have revealed that Tutankhamun's father was probably King Akhenaten and that his mother was most likely one of Akhenaten's lesser wives, Kiya. It was acceptable for kings to marry their sisters, and Tutankhamun himself married his half sister Ankhesenpaaten (she later became known as Ankhesenamun). Tests have also confirmed that two tiny mummies discovered in Tutankhamun's tomb were very likely his stillborn daughters.

The Aten Religion

Tutankhamun's father, Akhenaten, had
brought about a religious revolution in
Egypt. He had banned the traditional
gods in favor of a single god called Aten,
and had built a new capital city called
Akhetaten—"The Horizon of the Aten"
(modern day Amarna). However, when
Tutankhamun became pharaoh, this new
religion was abandoned. Thebes once
again became Egypt's capital and Amun-Ra
was restored as the most important god.

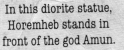

In this diorite statue,
Horemheb stands in
front of the god Amun.

The Reign of Horemheb

After four years, Ay was succeeded by Horemheb. He ruled
for 28 years, taking credit for much of Tutankhamun's
work in restoring order to Egypt, as well as for much of
his building work. It was in this way that the name of
Tutankhamun would become lost—for close to 3,000 years.

The Sealed Doors

Howard Carter's team resumed work on November 1, 1922. Three days later, the men removed the remains of some ancient work huts. As they cleared the rubble, imagine their excitement when a rock-cut step was uncovered. Could this be the entrance to a tomb?

The Hidden Staircase

The next day, 16 descending steps had been cleared and the top of a blocked doorway appeared. The door was covered with ancient seals, though they provided no clue as to who was buried inside. Despite his excitement, Carter ordered the staircase to be filled in again and sent a telegram summoning Carnarvon to Egypt.

This photograph shows the ancient seals on the mud plaster doorway.

4

The first sign of steps that descended to a blocked doorway.

"At last have made wonderful discovery in valley; a magnificent tomb with seals intact; re-covered same for your arrival; congratulations."
Howard Carter's telegram to Lord Carnarvon, November 6, 1922

The Pharaoh Named

On November 24, as Carnarvon looked on, the entire staircase was exposed. There were more seals on the lower part of the door. At last, Carter was able to read a name on the seals—Tutankhamun.

Sunday, November 26

Open second doorway
about 4 p.m.
Advised Engelbach.

After clearing 30 feet (9 m) of the descending passage, in about the middle of the afternoon, we came upon a second sealed doorway, which was almost the exact replica of the first. It bore similar seal impressions and had similar traces of successive reopenings and reclosings in the plastering. The seal impressions were of Tut.ankh.Amen and of the Royal Necropolis, but not in any way so clear as those on the first doorway. The entrance and passage both in plan and in style resembled almost to measurement the tomb containing the cache of Akhenaten discovered by Davis in the very near vicinity: which seemed to substantiate our first conjecture that we had found a cache.

Feverishly we cleared away the remaining last scraps of rubbish on the floor of the passage before the doorway, until we had only the clean sealed doorway before us. In which, after making preliminary notes, we made a tiny breach in the top left hand corner to see what was beyond. Darkness and the iron testing rod told us that there was empty space. Perhaps another descending staircase, in accordance to the ordinary royal Theban tomb plan? Or maybe a chamber...

This reconstruction of a page from Carter's journal details the lead up to the discovery of the first chamber.

Beyond the Sealed Door

The following day, Carter and his men cleared the debris around the door to reveal a downward sloping corridor. It was packed with limestone chips. After digging for about 30 feet (9 m), the men discovered a second blocked door also marked with the seals of Tutankhamun. But what lay beyond? On November 26, Carter began to break through the door...

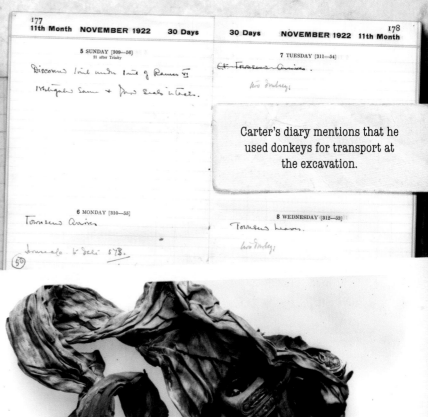

Carter's diary mentions that he used donkeys for transport at the excavation.

Burglars left behind this linen scarf in which eight gold rings had been wrapped.

Evidence of Burglary

As the men dug through the corridor, they found clear signs of burglary. Most of the corridor filling was white chips, but the top left-hand corner was made up of dark flint. This suggested a burglar's tunnel had been dug through and then refilled by valley officials who resealed the tomb. Additionally, the men found items, such as jewelry, among the chips. These had surely been dropped by fleeing burglars.

The Antechamber

Imagine yourself in Carter's shoes, standing at the doorway to Tutankhamun's tomb. A hole has been made in the door and you are about to look through it, though you have no idea what sight will greet your eyes. You light a candle and peer into the gloom. There, in the strange half-light, is a sight so extraordinary that at first you cannot take it in...

EXPLORE 360°

You have walked through the main tomb entrance and are standing in the Antechamber, facing southwest.

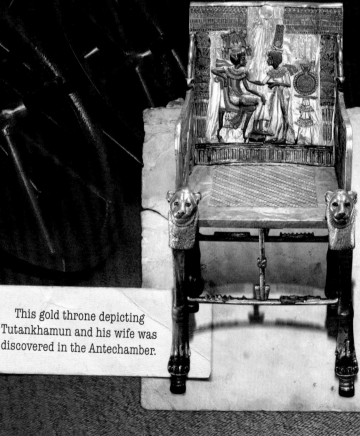

This gold throne depicting Tutankhamun and his wife was discovered in the Antechamber.

The Glint of Gold

Carter later wrote of how he was "struck dumb with amazement" when he first looked into the tomb. After several seconds, Carnarvon was unable to bear the suspense any longer and asked Carter if he could see anything. "Yes, wonderful things," came the stunned reply.

Objects piled up against the walls of the Antechamber.

Riches for the Afterlife

Three animal-headed beds lined the western wall of the room, probably intended to carry the dead pharaoh to the Afterlife. Beneath one of these was a gold throne, while underneath another were many white boxes containing joints of meat. Pieces of four chariots were lined up on the southeast wall. There was no sign of a coffin, but two life-size statues of Tutankhamun guarded another sealed doorway on the north wall. Carter soon realized that the room was an outer room (Antechamber)—the Burial Chamber must lie beyond the door.

"As my eyes grew accustomed to the light, details of the room within emerged slowly from the mist. Strange animals, statues, and gold— everywhere, the glint of gold."   Howard Carter

One of the scenes on the chest shows Tutankhamun in his chariot poised to fire arrows at his enemies.

The Painted Box

One of the first objects to be removed from the Antechamber was a beautiful chest painted with scenes showing Tutankhamun as a warrior and hunter. Carter considered this to be one of the tomb's finest treasures. The box contained items of the pharaoh's clothing, including robes decorated with gold, a fine linen glove, and sandals made of rush and papyrus.

Several pairs of sandals were found in the pharaoh's tomb. These are made with wood, leather, and gold foil.

33

You are standing
in the Burial
Chamber.
The room was
filled with the four
nested shrines.

The open doors of the
inner shrines that led to
Tutankhamun's sarcophagus
and coffins.

*"We bumped our heads, nipped our fingers;
we had to squeeze in and out like weasels, and
work in all kinds of embarrassing positions."*
Howard Carter

Gilded Shrines

Tutankhamun's shrines were eventually dismantled and
taken out in 51 parts. A burial cloth hung between the first
and second shrines. On the doors of the second shrine
were depictions of Tutankhamun before the gods Osiris
and Ra-Horakhty. Spells from *The Book of the Dead* were
inscribed on the third shrine. The doors of the innermost
shrine were guarded by the goddesses Isis and Nephthys,
while a wonderful carving of the goddess Nut, flanked by
the god Horus, gazed down from the ceiling.

This scene from the north wall depicts Tutankhamun being welcomed in his journey to the Afterlife by the goddess Nut.

Another part of the north wall shows Tutankhamun embraced by the god Osiris.

Painted Walls

The Burial Chamber was the only room in the tomb decorated with painted scenes. Set against a yellow background, the scenes show Tutankhamun's funeral, the pharaoh in the company of gods, and his arrival in the underworld. Some of the images are larger than those seen in other valley tombs— perhaps a sign that they were painted to cover the walls quickly after Tutankhamun's untimely death.

In the Presence of a Pharaoh

Once all the shrine doors had been opened, the excavators could see Tutankhamun's sarcophagus. Working conditions were difficult: the Burial Chamber was hot and stuffy, and space was tight. However, the doors of the second shrine were still sealed—and Carter now knew that surely Tutankhamun's mummy awaited them.

Into the Burial Chamber

Three months after the tomb was first opened, the time had come for the third sealed door to be broken through. The Antechamber had now been cleared of its exquisite treasures, and the excavation team—and an audience of selected guests—were about to find out if Tutankhamun's Burial Chamber really did lie behind the room's north wall.

Howard Carter and Lord Carnarvon stand in the excavated doorway to the Burial Chamber.

A Solid Wall of Gold

Carter and his team slowly began to dismantle the door. As the opening grew larger, the excavators saw what looked like a wall of solid gold decorated with mysterious symbols and inlaid with dazzling blue faience (glazed ceramic). Carter soon realized that the "wall" was in fact the side of a gilded shrine. Surely, it would contain the coffin of Tutankhamun?

The Death Mask

Instantly recognizable, Tutankhamun's extraordinary death mask is the most famous item from his tomb. Weighing about 22 pounds (10 kg), it is made of solid gold and inlaid with semi-precious stones and colored glass. The eyes are made of quartz and obsidian, with blue lapis lazuli representing the makeup the pharaoh would have worn in life.On the back of the mask are spells from *The Book of the Dead*.

The death mask was thought to give extra protection to the deceased and make him recognizable as a pharaoh.

2.

3.

The nested coffins
1. The outer coffin
2. The middle coffin
3. The inner coffin

The Outer Shrine

Though Carter didn't yet know it, Tutankhamun's Burial Chamber in fact housed four nested shrines that protected the pharaoh's sarcophagus. The first shrine was made of gilded oak and covered with protective symbols, including a pair of udjat-eyes. Alarmingly, its door was not sealed—it was still a possibility that tomb burglars had reached Tutankhamun's mummy.

The outer shrine was decorated with knotted amulets of the goddess Isis, representing protection.

A Glimpse of the Treasury

Once he had safely crawled inside the Burial Chamber, Carter invited his guests to do the same, three at a time. The shrine fitted the Burial Chamber tightly. On the chamber's east wall was an open door leading into what was later named the Treasury. Through it, the team glimpsed fascinating objects, such as model boats and another beautiful shrine (though it would be another three years before they would be examined).

A glimpse of the Treasury from a doorway in the Burial Chamber's east wall.

EXPLORE 360°

You are standing in the Antechamber looking toward the entrance of the Burial Chamber. You can see the wooden gilded shrine inside.

The Sarcophagus

Some experts believe that Tutankhamun's sarcophagus, carved from quartzite stone, may have originally been intended for another pharaoh. The red granite lid does not quite match the main body, and appears to have been added later. On February 12, 1924, Carter lifted the lid to reveal the first of the pharaoh's three human-shaped coffins.

The protective goddess Nephthys stands at one corner of the sarcophagus.

1.

"We felt that we were in the presence of the dead king and must do him reverence."
Howard Carter

Nested Coffins

Tutankhamun's beautiful coffins were extremely heavy, and a system of pulleys and ropes was used to lift them. The outermost coffin was made of gilded wood, and a wreath of olive leaves and flowers had been placed over the pharaoh's forehead. Also gilded, the second coffin had inlays of mainly colored glass, and was covered with a linen shroud and flower garlands. When the third coffin was revealed, the team was astounded to see it was made of solid gold, .12 inches (3 mm) thick. Its lid was finally lifted on October 28, 1925—at last, there was Tutankhamun's mummy, magnificently adorned with its now famous death mask.

The second coffin was inlaid with red and turquoise glass, faience (glazed ceramic), and semi-precious stones.

The Pharaoh's Mummy

Led by Professor Douglas Derry, the painstaking process of unwrapping Tutankhamun's corpse began in November 1925. The fragile mummy had become stuck to the coffin due to the resins used during the mummification process and had to be taken apart to be removed.

Tutankhamun Revealed

Carefully, the decayed wrappings were cut and removed—over 150 amulets and jewelry pieces were found among the bandages. Tutankhamun's mask was stuck fast to his head, and hot knives had to be used to detach it. At long last, Carter was able to see the 3,000-year-old face of the boy king. He described it as "serene and placid."

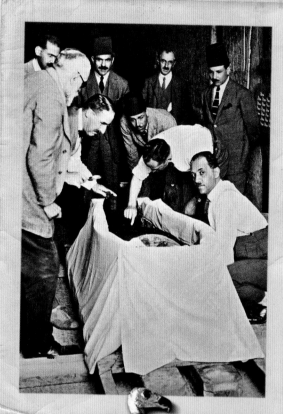

Douglas Derry and the team making an initial examination of the mummy's wrappings.

Carter and an Egyptian assistant cleaning the outside of the third coffin prior to finding the mummy.

This vulture pendant amulet was discovered among the mummy's inner wrappings.

AND
PAY SPOT CASH ON SIGHT
100 Cars Wanted at Once.
GEORGE NEWMAN & Co.
219-321, Euston Road, London, N.W.1
Phone Museum 1568, 1569 & 6675.

PALL MALL
GAZETTE AND GLOBE
London's Most Influential Evening Paper.

No. 18,045. [REGISTERED AT THE G.P.O. AS A NEWSPAPER]   THURSDAY, APRIL 5, 1923.   ONE PENNY.

LORD CARNARVON'S FATE.

EXPERTS AND A LUXOR "POISON TRAP."

SUPERSTITIOUS BELIEFS RIDICULED BY WELL-KNOWN EGYPTOLOGISTS.

TRAGEDY OF HIS DEATH.

EARL WHO FOUND TUTANKHAMEN'S TOMB, BUT NEVER SAW THE MUMMY.

The death of Lord Carnarvon, coming swiftly upon the heels of his great triumph—the discovery of the tomb of Pharaoh Tutankhamen in the Valley of the Kings—has created widespread controversy.

There will probably be thousands who see in the Earl's fate the "black arts" of the ancient Egyptians, while on the other hand the theory of a poison trap in the tomb is advanced.

Below, the "Pall Mall Gazette" publishes the views of well-known Egyptologists and pathologists, who ridicule, without exception, the theory that poison was left in the tomb for the purpose of dealing death to intruders.

Lord Carnarvon died peacefully in the early hours of this morning. He was conscious almost to the last.

The tragedy of his death lies in the fact that he never saw the mummy of the Pharaoh he discovered. He had deferred that for a year.

THOUGHT OF "VENGEANCE."

The Mummy's Curse

Just a few months after the discovery of Tutankhamun's tomb, Lord Carnarvon died as the result of an infected mosquito bite. Sadly, he never saw the pharaoh's incredible coffins or mask. Journalists lost no time in suggesting that there was an ancient curse at work. In reality, however, most people who entered the tomb lived to a good age, including Carter himself!

A CT scan of Tutankhamun's body stripped of its bandages.

The Postmortem

Tutankhamun's corpse was in poor condition—the skin was brittle, the nose had been squashed, and the ears were damaged. However, Derry was able to reveal that Tutankhamun had been about 5 feet 5 inches (1.65 m) tall, and that he had died at about the age of 18. There was evidence of several injuries, though the cause of death was unclear.

What Killed Tutankhamun?

Over the years, many theories have been put forward to explain Tutankhamun's sudden death, including murder or a chariot crash. In 2014, a "virtual autopsy" concluded that Tutankhamun had been severely weakened by genetic disabilities, and may have been unable to stand unaided. However, many disagree with this analysis.

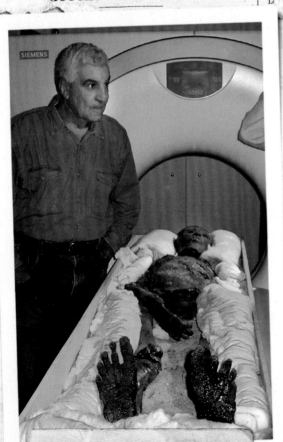

Zahi Hawass, head of the Egyptian Supreme Council of Antiquities, watches as the mummy undergoes a CT scan in 2005.

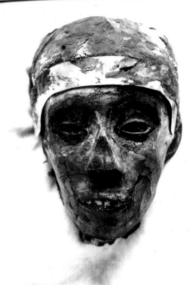

Tutankhamun's mummified head.

The Treasury

First glimpsed when the Burial Chamber was opened, the Treasury was found more or less undisturbed. The sight of the room's beautiful shrines, mysterious caskets, and glinting statues proved so distracting that Carter blocked the doorway until the team could begin to examine its extraordinary treasures in late 1926.

The Canopic Shrine

This lovely monument of gilded wood dominated the Treasury. Inside was a calcite chest decorated at each corner with gilded statues of the protective goddesses Isis, Nephthys, Neith, and Selket. The chest contained small coffinettes of beaten gold in which Tutankhamun's embalmed internal organs were held.

The Anubis Shrine

At the door to the Treasury stood a gilded shrine with a statue of the jackal god Anubis crouching on top. Painted black, the jackal's collar, ears, eye rims, and eyebrows are worked in gold leaf. The claws are inset with silver, which in ancient Egypt was more precious than gold. The shrine contained items possibly used during mummification.

EXPLORE 360°

You have come through the Burial Chamber and are looking east into the Treasury.

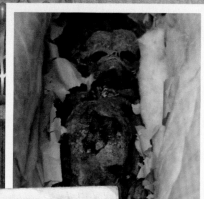

Mummified Children

Two tiny coffins were discovered in a wooden box. Inside each was a mummified fetus. They were the bodies of two small girls that had been born prematurely. They are almost certainly the children of Tutankhamun and his wife, Ankhesenamun.

The two mummified fetuses are now stored at the University of Cairo, Egypt.

Equipment for the Afterlife

The Treasury contained 18 model boats for Tutankhamun to use in the Afterlife. The Egyptians saw the sky as a heavenly river on which the sun god Ra traveled in his own boat. Some of these boats were for the pharaoh to sail across the heavens, while others were for river travel. The Treasury also contained many shabti figurines. These model servants were buried with wealthy Egyptians in the belief they would carry out difficult tasks for their masters in the Afterlife.

Like many ancient Egyptian tombs, Tutankhamun's contained model boats for use in the Afterlife.

"A single glance sufficed to tell us that here, within this little chamber, lay the greatest treasures of the tomb."
Howard Carter

These painted wooden shabti figures were discovered in the Treasury.

The Annex

On their first day in the tomb, Carter and Carnarvon had glimpsed the Annex—a small room adjoining the Antechamber—through a plunderer's hole in the wall. This storeroom was in such a state of chaos that they decided to postpone examining it until the rest of the tomb had been cleared—almost five years later.

The small door leading from the Antechamber to the Annex.

Jumbled Artifacts

Tomb burglars had broken through the door leading to the Annex and jumbled objects were stacked nearly 6 feet (1.8 m) high in places. In total, the chamber contained nearly 2,000 items, including reed baskets and pottery jars containing oil, food, and wine for the dead pharaoh. Although the Annex was intended as a provisions storeroom, haste and lack of space meant that furniture had also been placed inside.

The Mark of a Thief

Because the crammed Annex was so small, only one burglar would have been able to enter it at a time. He probably rifled through the objects, hastily emptying containers and passing artifacts through the hole to his companions, while throwing other items aside. Carter discovered the thief's 3,000-year-old dirty footprints on the lid of a white box.

The burglar's footprints were clearly visible on a white box.

Calcite Boat

One of the items discovered in the Annex was this richly decorated calcite vessel with ibex heads at each end. Its precise function continues to baffle Egyptologists —perhaps it was an ointment or cosmetics jar, or it may have been purely ornamental. The boat is like a funeral bark, and the central carving appears to be an open sarcophagus.

The ornamental calcite boat had ibex heads on the prow and stern.

EXPLORE 360°

You are standing in the Annex facing west.

"He had done his work just as about as thoroughly as an earthquake."

Carter, writing about the tomb burglar

The Team at Work

The task of clearing and recording Tutankhamun's tomb was huge. Each object had to be accurately recorded before it could be removed, and the utmost care had to be taken to protect the priceless treasures. It took Carter's skilled team 10 years to unpack the tomb.

Keeping Records

Before anything was touched, skilled photographer Harry Burton photographed each room of the tomb in detail. This was difficult work, as the chambers were cramped with no natural light. Numbered cards were then placed on each object, and the rooms photographed again and detailed plans drawn. This meant that the exact position of every object was clear, and that each could be identified by a number. Carter made precise drawings of many of the artefacts, and detailed notes were kept describing all the finds.

One of Harry Burton's photographs showing numbered objects in the Antechamber.

"It was slow work... and nerve-wracking at that."
Howard Carter

Carter and his team made detailed plans of the tomb. This one shows the Antechamber.

Removing the Treasures

The process of removing the tomb's contents would have been impossible without a large workforce of local men and boys. Objects were carried out on padded stretchers for treatment in the nearby tomb of Sety II, which served as a "laboratory." The conservation work was largely carried out by archaeologist Arthur Mace and a chemist and conservator Alfred Lucas.

Arthur Mace (left) and Alfred Lucas (right) inspect a chariot found in the tomb.

A funerary bouquet made with olive leaves being removed from the tomb.

This scarab beetle bracelet is still housed at the Egyptian Museum in Cairo.

To Cairo

Once this vital work was complete, the objects were packed into crates and transported to the Egyptian Museum in Cairo by means of a specially constructed Decauville railway. Wheeled trucks had to be pushed by hand for 5.4 miles (9 km)—in the blistering heat of summer—toward the Nile. Here, waiting boats shipped the tomb's treasures to their final destination.

Tutankhamun's Legacy

Today, Tutankhamun's mummy once again lies in its Valley of the Kings tomb (KV62). Millions of visitors have descended through the tomb's sloping corridor to stand in the dead pharaoh's presence.

Treasures on Display

However, the four chambers that make up Tutankhamun's tomb were supposed to remain sealed forever. Unfortunately, decades of tourism have taken their toll. Moisture has damaged the tomb's murals and wall cracks are expanding. For this reason, a replica tomb has now been built near Luxor, recreating every little detail of the original.

Almost all the objects from the tomb are housed in the Egyptian Museum in Cairo. All the original photographs and records made by Howard Carter and his team are kept at the Griffith Institute, Oxford University and are available for all to view online. Less than half of Tutankhamun's treasures have been fully studied. They surely have much more to tell us about ancient Egypt.

Tutankhamun's sarcophagus—part of the replica of the tomb now open at Luxor.

Howard Carter and his team's painstaking work has left us treasures to enjoy for generations to come.

Tourists visiting Tutankhamun's tomb at the Valley of the Kings in 2006.